LET'S LOOK AT CATS

LET'S LOOK AT CATS

by Harriet E. Huntington

Doubleday & Company, Inc., Garden City, New York

Library of Congress Cataloging in Publication Data

Huntington, Harriet E.
Let's Look at Cats.

Summary:
An introduction to all the genera of cats, from wild to domestic.
1. Cats—Juvenile literature.   2. Felidae—
Juvenile literature.   [1. Cats.   2. Felidae]
I. Title.
SF445.7.H86   5.99.74'428
AACR2

Library of Congress Catalog Card Number 80-707
ISBN: 0-385-14858-5 Trade
0-385-14859-3 Prebound

First Edition

CONTENTS

LET'S LOOK AT CATS

Introduction

Let's look at cats. We usually think of a cat as being a pet, living with its owner. Cats have not lived with humans as long as dogs have. They probably were domesticated by the Egyptians who discovered that cats killed rats, which ate harvested and stored grain. Ever since, cats have been helpful in keeping the rat and mouse population somewhat under control. However, as pets, cats are very independent. They do not stay with their owners as constant companions the way dogs do but like to go off on their own— hunting or protecting their territory. To understand and appreciate the domestic cat, it helps to know about the behavior of their ancestors—the big cats.

Cats can live almost anywhere in the world except the very cold countries surrounding the icy Arctic. Strangely, there are no indigenous (native born) cats in Australia, New Zealand, Madagascar, or the West Indies.

Some wildcats, such as the bobcat of North America and the common wildcat of Europe, Asia, and Russia are only slightly larger than the domesticated animal. But most cats from the wild are considerably larger, such as lions, tigers, leopards, cheetahs, which live in Africa, Asia, India, and China; or jaguars, cougars, and pumas which live in North and South America.

You can see some of these big cats in zoos and circuses; the domesticated kind often turns feral or semiwild and roams or runs loose on the city streets, while many beautiful and popular varieties of domestic cats, such as the Siamese and Persian, are exhibited at cat shows.

To classify the cats, the cat family (Felidae) had been divided into three subgroups or genera. The scientific names for these genera are: *Leo, Acinonyx,* and *Felis.* Each genus is made up of one or more species. Although all cats have very much the same body structure, those species which share bodily characteristics not common to the others are placed in a separate genus.

For example because the cheetah is the only cat whose claws are not retractable, but remain extended, like a dog's, it is the only species that comprises the genus *Acinonyx*.

The genus *Felis* contains small to medium-sized wildcats as well as domestic and show cats.

Because of the way in which the cat's bones and connecting joints are placed, the cat can execute movements that are both agile and most helpful in hunting and general survival. For instance, the cat is capable of several different gaits—slow alternating movements of the legs when stalking and walking, moving front and rear feet together when loping at a fast gallop, and also like the camel, moving both feet on the same side at the same time when trotting at a moderate pace.

The hip ball-and-socket joint allows the cat to have great agility in climbing and jumping. The elbow on the front legs is somewhat like the one in your arm. It has a hinge joint which permits the cat to take a swinging, batting, or swiping motion. This permits the cat, if hunting, to swipe at its prey, or if playing, to hit and start a ball rolling.

The neck has two pivotal joints or special vertibrae bones between the neck bones which allow the head to turn from side to side. It also permits the cat to lick itself on any part of the body, except at the back of its head and between its shoulder blades.

The cat's tail is an extension of its spinal column. Thus it can move in all directions. The tail helps the cat balance itself when climbing or leaping, and to right itself when falling. In a long fall, as it starts descending with its feet above, a cat is able by a flick of its tail to turn itself over and to land on all four feet.

One of the important characteristics of most cats is the ability to retract the claws.

(Gale M. Adler)

The claw is at the tip of each toe and it is retracted into a kind of pocket or sheath above the toe pad. If the cats are climbing trees, fighting, defending themselves, killing prey or tearing it apart, the claws are extended. If the claws are not in use they are drawn back into the sheath to protect and keep them sharp. When a cat sharpens its claws by scratching the bark of trees, furniture, or a scratching post, it pulls off the worn outer layer of the claw and exposes the new, sharp underlayer.

Unlike the eyes of a horse or cow, which are placed at the side of its head, the eyes of the cat, like those of hunting mammals, are placed side by side at the front of its head. Part of what one eye sees overlaps part of what the other eye sees. This produces good depth perception, enabling the cat to judge distances and the speed of the prey. A cat can move its eyes from side to side and up and down so that it does not have to turn its head. This is important when the cat is hunting or stalking prey because the movement of the head could attract the attention of the prey and frighten it away.

All cats, except the genus *Leo*, have pupils that in strong sunlight become vertical slits rather than contract into smaller round pupils as human eyes do. The cat also has eyes that are especially geared to detecting movements. In fact, a cat might look straight at a mouse but not notice it because the mouse was not moving. Cats, like most mammals, are color blind and see colors as different shades of gray—similar to a black and white photograph.

Inside the eye there is a special layer of cells which enable the cat to see in very dim light. The layer acts like a mirror and reflects surrounding light back and out of the eye. This is what makes the cat's eyes shine or glow in the dark.

The cat's tongue is covered with small protuberances called papillae. One might think of them as being like the bristles of a brush, only very, very short bristles. As the cat licks its paws or fur, the papillae remove dirt, dust, or small particles of food. Domestic cats, and the big cats as well, use their tongues for grooming and gestures of affection. A big cat's tongue is proportionately larger than the domestic cat's tongue and the larger papillae can scrape bones clean of meat and gristle.

Like all carnivores, or meat-eating animals, cats have four large canine teeth which are used for stabbing while killing prey and also for tearing meat from a carcass.

To catch sounds, cats can aim or turn their ears in the direction from where the sound is coming. The cat can hear high-pitched sounds that our ears are unable to detect.

(Gale M. Adler)

13

GENUS LEO
LION

At one time the lion, *Leo Leo* (until recently classified as *Panthera leo*) populated countries around the Mediterranean Sea and India. Today, lions live in the central and southern parts of Africa and only a few remain in the Gir forest of north India. Most of the lions, approximately two thousand, live in the five-thousand-square-mile Serengeti National Park which is not far south of the equator and near the east coast of Africa. The park has a varied landscape—from grassy plains and sparsely wooded valleys to thick forests.

The average male lion measures about nine feet long and weighs from four-hundred to five-hundred pounds. In the animal world the male is generally larger than the female. Lionesses are about eight feet long and weigh about three-hundred pounds.

One can tell a male from a female lion because the male generally has a mane which looks somewhat like a ruff or wide collar, while a female does not. A lion's mane does not grow down the back of his neck like a horse's mane. Instead, it covers all but the face of the head, encircles the neck, and stops at the shoulders. Because the brownish hairs are long, about six inches, the mane hangs down in front of his chin somewhat like a bib. The purpose of the mane is to intimidate any predator by making the lion look larger than he actually is. It also protects the lion's neck from his enemy's teeth.

Both male and female lions have dark brown tufts of hair at the tip of their tails, and the back of their ears is also dark brown. Their fur coats range in color from a rich tan to a golden brown. The underside of their bellies and the inside of their legs are off-white. This creates a camouflage, because it lightens what otherwise would be in shadow. Therefore, instead of being sil-

(San Diego Zoo)

houetted against the background, the lion blends into it. The light fur also deflects heat especially when the lion rests on its back.

Lions have large whiskers which grow in parallel horizontal rows above the lips under the nose and to the side. One might think of the rows as being like a mustache. At the base of each whisker is a dark spot. There is also a top row of spots without whiskers and it is the position of these spots in relation to the position of the spots with whiskers in the row below that creates a pattern. These patterns vary with each lion and can be a method of identifying the individual lions. However, if the lion population is large, such as in the Serengeti Park, there may be duplications.

Unlike other cats, lions live and hunt together in prides. You might think of a pride as being a kind of family. There can be from two to thirty-five lions in a pride, which consists mainly of lionesses, their cubs, and at least one mature male lion. The average pride contains about seven adult females and two adult males with a variable number of cubs. A lioness usually has from two to four cubs in a litter but she may have from one to even six. When the cubs are first born they are spotted, but as they grow older the spots become lighter until they are very faint and are scarcely noticeable. Occasionally, when a pride becomes too large, some of the female two-year-old cubs are made to leave. Unable to hunt alone successfully, they die of starvation.

When a mature male grows old and begins to lose his strength, his ability to retain his position in the pride is challenged by a younger male. A battle occurs between the two, and if the younger one wins, the older lion leaves.

The lionesses in each pride are almost always related to each other—either as mothers, daughters, sisters, aunts, or cousins. This is because they were born into and remained with the pride. Very seldom do lionesses join another pride. Usually they leave because they are too old to be useful— they no longer are strong enough to hunt successfully or to protect the cubs from predators such as jackals.

(San Diego Zoo)

The mature male lions are not related to the lionesses, having grown up in a different pride. They had left their own prides when they were young adults and capable of fending for themselves. These young males lived a nomadic life for about two years until they were able to enter a pride by successfully challenging an older male. These unrelated males keep the bloodline from deteriorating through interbreeding. In other words, the male does not mate with his sister, mother, aunt, or cousin and thereby restrict the variability of the gene pool. The unrelated males bring different genes to keep the bloodline healthy.

Like many cats, lions hunt more at night than in the daytime. It is the lioness' job to do the hunting for the pride. On the open plains where the zebras and wildebeests live in herds, a group of lions will work together. The lionesses encircle the rear of a herd while the male or another lioness at the front of the herd will grunt and make attacking movements. They frighten the prey so they will then stampede toward the waiting female lions.

In the scarcely populated tree and bush country, the lionesses hunt singly. They stalk or ambush their prey—zebra, wildebeest, impala, gazelle, or warthogs. Sometimes they wait half a day hidden in the brush at a water hole. A large kill, such as an impala, is often fought for by the male, who usually appropriates it, or by a stronger female, as well as by some two-year-old cubs. However, at times a lioness is able to bring her young cubs to feed upon her kill unmolested by the other members of her pride. After a lion kill, scavenging jackals and vultures gather around the carcass but wait until the lions have finished.

Lions do a lot of sleeping and resting. In fact, they are active, moving about for only four hours of the day. When it is very hot they will seek whatever shade they can find, lie still, and at times pant gently.

Aside from mating with the lionesses, the male lion's job is to mark the pride's hunting territory. This territory remains the same size from one generation of lionesses to another. Pride territories can be from ten to forty square miles. If the pride is large,

(Lion Country Safari)

the lionesses often form groups and each group has its own portion of the whole.

The boundaries between neighboring prides are not exact, such as a river, or a cliff. Instead, there is a buffer zone or no-man's-land between the two territories. Lions as a rule avoid going into their neighbor's land. Usually each territory contains enough prey to satisfy the hunger of the pride throughout the year. By restricting the use of the land to members and by driving out intruders, a pride can remain permanently in the same territory.

Usually male lions mark the pride's territory with their urine. There are two methods of doing this. One is for the lion to approach a bush or small tree which has some head high branches. He sniffs the leaves and rubs his head into them. After this he turns around so that his rear end is close to the bush, lifts his tail, and in a series of sprays ejects his urine onto the leaves. The other and more common way is for the lion to eject urine onto his back feet while he alternately scrapes the ground. This not only marks the spot but leaves a scent trail. As he moves over the territory, the area is permeated with a slight odor. A trespassing lion would have no doubt that the territory was occupied.

Another way lions keep other lions from trying to enter or settle in their territory is by roaring. A lion's roar is very loud and upon a quiet night can be heard five miles away. Usually, a group of females, cubs, and males lying about in a group resting will start a chorus of roars. At first they make a low moaning sound which is followed by a louder one. Then there is a succession of pure roars in which the males join. Frequently after the last sound fades away into silence, a neighboring pride replies with their chorus of roars. Male lions roar more frequently than the females, particularly when they patrol the territory.

(San Diego Zoo)

LEOPARD
Leo pardus

In the same African environment lives the leopard, *Leo pardus* (until recently classified as *Panthera pardus*). However, this big cat also inhabits Asia, India, China, and Manchuria. In fact, it has a larger population and is more widely distributed than any other of the big cats. Leopards live from sea level to high altitudes, from semidesert stream beds to the rain forest; and from the warm tropics to the cold Arctic.

The average leopard is about eight feet from the tip of its nose to the end of its two- or three-foot long tail and weighs from eighty to two-hundred pounds. Leopardesses are about one third smaller. The leopard is covered with dark brown, almost black, spots. These spots so blend with patches of sunlight or moonlight, and with shadows under trees, that the animal is often completely camouflaged. Each leopard spot, called a rosette, is composed of five

small dots that form a circle. Their center is darker than the animal's overall tan-colored fur. Around the leopard's face are single spots that become smaller near the nose and eyes. These spots vary in number and position so that no two face patterns are alike. It is by these distinctive patterns that individual leopards can be recognized.

The underside of the leopard's tail is white. When walking through the thick and high grass the female leopard will hold her tail up, using it as a flag for her cubs to see and to follow.

Leopards live a solitary existence except when they are mating or the female is taking care of her young cubs. They do not hunt in teams as lions do, nor do they hunt as much during the daytime. They are more nocturnal. Leopards either stalk or ambush their prey. When stalking they move slowly, seeking cover from one bush to another. If the

(Joseph Fadler)

prey notices any movement, hears any sound, or smells the leopard, it will stop feeding, look up, alert and ready to flee from danger. At the same time the leopard freezes, and stays still until the prey relaxes and resumes feeding. The leopard depends upon its swift attack to catch its prey. It can dash suddenly, leap ten or more feet into the air and pull the prey down with its claws. Then the leopard immediately bites the victim's neck aiming to crunch the spinal cord and thereby kill the animal.

After killing the prey, the leopard will usually take it up into a nearby tree, out of reach of scavengers, such as hyenas. Leopards have very strong necks and can easily carry in their mouths gazelles and impalas that weigh almost as much as they do. The leopard takes from two to three days to finish eating a gazelle or impala. Leopards are also scavengers of larger animals, such as giraffes, buffaloes, zebras, and hartebeests that die from old age, starvation, or other natural causes.

Although they take their kill up into the safety of the tree or take naps draped over shaded limbs—the leopards seldom, if ever, use the tree as ambush—to drop down upon an animal. However, leopards have been known to chase a single baboon in and among the branches of a tree and if one dropped to the ground the leopard would follow and being larger could catch and kill it quickly. Incidentally, a leopard will attack only a lone baboon. The leopard is afraid of a group of baboons that could attack and kill him.

When ambushing, leopards hide in bushes near water holes or near paths frequented by their prey. The leopard will flush or scare out from bushes a hare or dik-dik, a small antelope, then dash, leap after the fleeing animal, and sometimes catch it—but not often. Being a typical cat, the leopard also will flush birds from a clump of grass. However, birds quickly fly out of reach.

(San Diego Zoo)

TIGER
Leo tigris

There are two major subspecies of tigers—the Siberian, *Leo tigris altaica,* and the Bengal, *Leo tigris tigris* (until recently classified respectively *Panthera tigris altaica* and *Panthera tigris tigris).* The Siberian tiger is the largest of the big cats. It measures twelve feet long, including its three-foot tail, and weighs about seven hundred pounds. As its name implies, it lives in the northern icy forests of Siberia and Manchuria. These tigers are larger and have a lighter yellow-and-brown-colored fur coat than those that live in the southern tropical countries of India, Burma, Thailand, the Malay Peninsula, and the Javanese islands. As protection from the cold snow and ice the Siberian tigers have a thick and long-haired coat.

The Bengal tigers are small, weighing about three hundred pounds. They have a short-haired coat. The Bengal tiger has a darker orange to reddish brown or tawny coat with black stripes. When a tiger is in the tall, dry, orange-yellow grass, the animal is almost invisible. Even when it is in the shadow-filled dark rain forests and jungles it is difficult to see. Colors tend to be lighter in the northern snowbound countries and darker in the southern, dense-forested countries. In this way the coats blend into the landscape.

Both tigers have approximately the same stripe pattern of rich dark brown or black lines. These are vertical on the body, starting at the ridge of the spine and going over and down the sides. The tail is ringed, as are the hind legs. The underside of the Bengal tiger is paler than the body, similar to the camouflage of the lion. Both have a white spot on the back of their black ears. Both have pink noses and yellow-amber-colored eyes.

(San Diego Zoo)

(San Diego Zoo)

Like leopards, Bengal tigers are solitary hunters except for the two weeks in the spring or winter when they are mating. Being nocturnal, tigers wait until it is dark before going out to hunt. However, if they are very hungry they will hunt in the daytime. Camouflaged by its stripes and hidden among the branches of bushes or high grass, the tiger silently and slowly stalks its prey until it is close enough to rush and knock it down. Almost simultaneously it bites the throat and often breaks the neck of its victim.

Tigresses live with and hunt for their young until the cubs are able to fend for themselves. Sometimes, after leaving the mother, the cubs will stay for a time with each other. Then the male cub kills prey for his sisters. Although the tigers do not live together as in a pride, a tigress will share its kill with another tiger. There is no bickering or fighting, like lions, over a kill. While male tigers will allow females and cubs to feed upon his kill, they do not as a rule tolerate another male's doing so.

Bengal tigers will eat almost any animal—water buffaloes, wild oxen, cows, deer, bears, monkeys, pigs, badgers, wolves, lynxes, lizards, frogs, fish, and locusts. They will also eat carrion. Man-eating tigers are scarce.

Depending upon the size of the kill, the tiger may eat it up in a couple of hours. However, if the catch is a large one it will take it near water so that it may drink as it eats, or it may stand guard over it and take a couple of days to consume it.

The tiger enjoys diving into rivers and ponds just to swim. During the hot weather, when it wishes to escape from the heat, it will remain immersed up to its neck and soak for hours lying near the edge of ponds and lakes. Tigers have been known to swim from one Javanese island to another in search of food.

In circuses tigers are trained to ride on a platform slung over the back of an elephant. They, like lions, also perform with their trainer in the circus ring.

In their natural habitat, tigers sleep in trees, draped over a limb above the ground. The tiger in the picture opposite was photo-

(Harriet E. Huntington)

graphed at the Gentle Jungle, Riverside, California. It is resting on a shelf that substitutes for a large limb while the shade from the protecting roof substitutes for that of a tall jungle tree. The Gentle Jungle is a kind of zoo. However, the animals are also used as actors in motion pictures and television shows. They have been trained from cubs and having been taught with affection and praise they are not vicious or mean. In fact, they are treated and react as pets. The tigers rub their heads against their trainers, somewhat in the same manner as domestic cats rub against the legs of their owners to show affection. Tigers do not purr but do make sounds of greeting and pleasure. Although the animals within the Gentle Jungle have been tamed to a certain degree, the trainers know how to control them if they revert to type and become wild, temporarily.

Many people have thought and still think it would be fun to own a wild cat. They will go out and buy a lion, tiger, cheetah, ocelot, serval, or caracal cub. The cub is very cute and for a few months everything seems to be all right. But as the cub begins to grow, problems arise and not having been taught to handle the wild animal, the owner usually ends up with an unmanageable cat that has become a tremendous problem. Then the cat has to be disposed of and this usually is to a local zoo, which is probably overpopulated with cats. Because this has happened so frequently, most states have enacted laws that limit importation, sale, purchase, and ownership of wild cats.

(Harriet E. Huntington)

JAGUAR
Leo onca

The jaguar, *Leo onca* (until recently classified as *Panthera onca*), is another cat that roars. Because the jaguar was the only animal that could let out a bloodcurdling sound, it was no wonder that the ancient civilizations of Peru, Central America, and Mexico made the animal a god. Even its name carried a feeling of fear and awe. Jaguar comes from the ancient Indian name *yaguar* which is believed to mean "the killer which overcomes its prey in one leap." Along with other big cats, jaguars have been known to kill humans, but it is not certain that they become man-eaters.

The jaguar inhabits the jungles of Mexico, Central America, and the northern half of South America, especially Brazil. The cat is marked with small solid spots on its large head, lower legs, and paws, as well as large spots, especially on its tail. However, its rosettes are larger than the leopard's and are composed of five or six spots with an extra one in the dark yellow or tawny center. Slightly shorter and stockier than the leopard, the jaguar is approximately seven or more feet in length including its tail, and it weighs from two hundred fifty to four hundred pounds.

Although the jaguar will eat almost any kind of animal, it feeds mainly upon the peccary, a kind of wild pig, and the capybara, a large aquatic tailless rodent which measures four feet in length and weighs around one hundred pounds. Near and on the shore of rivers the cat hunts for caiman, a South American alligator. The cat jumps on the alligator, usually kills it by breaking its neck, and with its powerful paws tears away its thick, scaly skin to get at the flesh. If the jaguar lives close to the Atlantic Ocean, it hunts turtles near the shore. To kill these, it first turns the turtle over onto its back, then rips it out of its shell. Sometimes it will search in the sand along the beach for turtle eggs.

The jaguar does not dislike water. Often it will leap into ponds, lakes, or rivers to swim after alligator, turtle, or fish. The cat is also very much at home in the trees and will chase monkeys from branch to branch.

(San Diego Zoo)

SNOW LEOPARD and
CLOUDED LEOPARD *Leo uncia and Leo nebulosa*

The snow leopard, *Leo uncia* (until recently classified *Panthera uncia),* has spots which are somewhat similar to those of a leopard, which is probably one reason why this cat was given the common name of leopard. However, the spots, instead of being definite rosettes, are more like irregular splashes of dark tan outlined by dark brown borders on a pale gray, white, or light yellowish buff coat. This coat grows longer and thicker in winter. The white hairs on its underside are longer than those at its sides and on its back. They act as insulation against the icy snow when the cat lies down and curls up to sleep. There are small solid spots on its head and lower parts of its legs. On the upper side of its bushy tail are larger spots. The snow leopard is about four feet long, the tail is about three feet and it weighs from 100 to 180 pounds. The snow leopard, as the name implies, lives in the cold mountains in central Russia, Afghanistan, India, Tibet, Mongolia, and western China, at altitudes ranging from 12,000 to 18,000 feet above sea level.

The clouded leopard, *Leo nebulosa* (until recently classified as *Panthera nebulosa),* has smallish, irregular dark brown spots on its front and back legs with larger ones on its tail. Its body has dark tan blotches outlined by both dark brown and by light tan borders. The coloring of the background coat can vary from gray or brown to yellow, while the underside is white. The clouded leopard's tail, which measures from 2½ to 3 feet, is almost as long as its body, which can measure from 3 to 3½ feet. It weighs about fifty pounds. Because the clouded leopard inhabits the dense forests of Southeast Asia and Indonesia, it spends most of its time up in the trees. It hunts small animals and birds in the early dawn hours and then again in the late afternoon or evening hours. Neither the clouded leopard or the snow leopard is a true leopard; nor can either be classified as either a big cat or a small cat. They have some characteristics of both.

SNOW LEOPARD (San Diego Zoo)

CLOUDED LEOPARD (San Diego Zoo)

GENUS ACINONYX
CHEETAH

A cheetah, *Acinonyx jubatus*, looks more like a racing dog than a cat. Its extra long legs, narrow body, small head, and supple backbone enable it to run swiftly. In fact, the cheetah is the fastest mammal on earth. Within two seconds it can attain the speed of forty-five miles per hour and can maintain up to seventy miles per hour for a short distance, about a quarter of a mile. However, the cheetah does not have the endurance to keep up the fast pace and if it is chasing an impala it must get a good start to be able to knock it down. Because they do not have long canine teeth, cheetahs will bite the prey under its throat and thus strangle it.

The cheetah does not have retractable claws like other cats and therefore cannot climb trees. The foot pads are ridged, not rounded, which helps the cat to have a firmer foothold. You might think of the claws as being like the cleats of hiking boots. They dig into the ground, enabling the cat to have a firm foothold so that it can run swiftly, as well as turn quickly changing direction or swerve around a bush or rock.

Like the greyhound, it can bend its spine to run a double-suspension gallop. In this gallop the cat leaps so that it can extend both its front and rear legs at the same time and create the first suspension. Then the cat will leap so that it can arch its back so both its front and rear feet are tucked under its belly while it is traveling forward through the air. This is the second suspension. As long as the gallop continues, one suspension follows the other.

Because of their ability to run swiftly, cheetahs were trained by ancient sultans and maharajas of Assyria, India, and Central Asia to course or race over the countryside after animals.

(San Diego Zoo)

Cheetahs are easily distinguished from other large cats because they have a characteristic dark "tear" streak which goes from the inside of the eye to the outer edge of its mouth. As with leopards, the identifying spots on each side of the face are not identical. The cheetah does not have rosettes. Instead, it has various sizes of solid black spots scattered all over its body.

Cheetahs live on the eastern side of Africa and mainly in the open grassy plains of the Serengeti National Park. Because cheetahs follow the migratory herds of gazelles, they do not seem to have any strong inclination or need to claim territorial rights.

The cats are diurnal, moving about and hunting during the daytime. Hunting on the plains. they have no way to store a large kill so they could continue to eat it the next day. In fact, they do not eat meat unless it has been freshly killed. They eat their fill, leave the carcass for scavengers, and hunt again the next day. They have good fortune in their ability to kill prey; they are successful half the time.

Although it is a cat, the cheetah yelps like a dog. However, cheetahs purr like cats and make birdlike chirping sounds when separated from each other.

There is no special breeding season near the equator, as the climate is almost always warm. The gestation period is three months and the litter contains from two to four cubs. When the cubs are newly born, their heads and backs have a kind of extra coat of white hair that is long and fuzzy. This probably is a kind of camouflage and makes them seem larger and therefore not so vulnerable. After they are three or four months old the mother takes them along to learn how to hunt. Cheetahs are not social and do not live in prides like lions. When four or five cheetahs are seen together it is probably a mother with her full-grown cubs. When the cubs are about two years old they leave their mother, find a mate, and begin their solitary life.

GENUS FELIS
PUMA

The genus *Felis* has the most, about thirty or more, species, and contains the small to medium-sized wild cats as well as all the domestic cats. The puma, *Felis concolor*, is the largest cat of the genus *Felis* and one of the largest cats in both North and South America. Measuring eight feet, the puma is a foot longer than the jaguar but weighs less, about half as much, or two hundred pounds. In other words, it is not stocky, although its longish, thick coat gives an impression of bigness. Those inhabiting the mountain ranges of the Sierras and Andes are larger than those living in the deserts and jungles. These are about two feet shorter, measuring six feet, and weigh about half as much, or, one hundred pounds.

Although they meet infrequently, the jaguars and pumas are enemies. The puma is usually able to escape from the jaguar because of its agility and swiftness. From a stationary position the puma can readily leap twenty-five feet when attacking its prey.

The puma resembles the African lioness, but the males have no manes. The coat is a solid golden grayish tan color. The underside of the body, throat, and inner side of the legs are whitish, while the backs of the ears are dark brown and the tip of the tail is black. Even the eyes are the same tawny color—an orange-reddish yellow. It is easy to understand why it is called a mountain lion. Occasionally it is called a catamount, which is an abbreviation for "cat-a-mountain." It also has been named panther and cougar.

The puma has adapted itself to the habits of its prey. In the mountains up to ten thousand feet above sea level, it hunts diurnally, as the white-tailed deer and mountain elk feed during the daytime. Unlike the cheetah, which leaves the carcass of its kill for scavengers, the puma will bury its prey in the snow or under a bush. In the lowlands it hunts nocturnally, since the animals it eats are active at night; a large puma may travel twenty or twenty-five miles in one night.

(Los Angeles Zoo)

CARACAL
Felis caracal

The caracal, *Felis caracal*, is about three feet long and weighs about thirty to thirty-five pounds. You might think of caracals as being middle-size cats—not as large as the big cats nor as small as the small wild or domestic cats. Caracals live in dry and hilly parts of Asia, India, and most of Africa from the Mediterranean Sea to the Cape of Good Hope.

A caracal's ears are black with black tufts at their tips. In Turkish the word caracal means "black-eared." The tufts, as you can see in the picture on the opposite page, are quite large and have a number of long black hairs. These hairs act as a kind of antennae and help the cat to have acute hearing. Because of the lynxlike ear tufts, the caracal also is called the African lynx. However, the lynx and the caracal are not the same species.

The caracal's unmarked shorthaired coat is a reddish brown color, while its whitish underbelly sometimes is spotted with brown. It also has white around its mouth, under its chin, and at the edge of its greenish eyes near the nose and cheeks. Unfortunately, the caracals were once hunted extensively for their fur and nearly became extinct. Now they are protected by game laws.

In India and Iran the caracal was trained to hunt like the cheetah. While the cheetah stalked large antelope, the caracal, also a very fast runner, hunted small gazelles and flushed game birds. The caracal eats birds more than any other prey, and is proficient at catching them. The cat leaps and grabs the bird with one or both paws while at the same time bringing it to its mouth so as to bite and kill it. Often caracals will attack a flock of birds feeding on the ground. The cat will dash into their midst, swipe at them as they take flight, and sometimes kill as many as eight or ten. The agile caracal climbs trees in search of or to reach nesting and roosting birds.

(Los Angeles Zoo)

LYNX and BOBCAT
Felis lynx and *Felis rufa*

Sometimes called Canadian or northern lynx, the lynx, *Felis lynx*, inhabits the countries bordering on the Arctic Circle—Alaska, Canada, northern Europe, and Russia. A few lynx have been found in the northern New England states—Maine, New Hampshire, Vermont, upper New York, around the Great Lakes, and as far south as Colorado.

The paws of the lynx are large and covered with thick hairs. They act somewhat like snowshoes and enable it to walk or run on top of soft snow without sinking. It has tufts at the tip of its ears which act as antennae or amplifiers. These tufts are important, because snow deadens the sound of footfalls, and the lynx depends very much upon its ears to locate its prey. It has been discovered that if the tufts are cut off, the cat's hearing ability is diminished.

The longish hairs around the neck could be called a ruff but it is not as prominent a one as that of the lion. Lynx fur is thick and has long gray guard hairs that form a protective coating over the underfur. The dark gray markings do not have clear-cut lines but blend into the pale tannish-gray coat. The lynx weighs forty pounds and has strong hind legs and a shortish tail.

The cat will stake out a territory, marking caves, rocks and trees by droppings and claw marks. Although males will allow other males to enter, females are more particular. If another female accidently enters, she is challenged and sent running for safety. The lynx hunts alone and shuns contact with other lynx except during the mating season in early spring. Then the woods resound with the yowls of the males.

A subspecies of lynx lives in Spain, and

from the western part of the Mediterranean Sea east to Asia. These cats, often called Spanish or European lynx, are colored yellowish-red with black spots, splotches, and lines. The tail is short with a black tip.

The bobcat, *Felis rufa*, lives only on the North American continent from Mexico into the southern half of Canada. Because the word "bob" means to cut shorter and because the bobcat has a shorter tail than the majority of cats, the cat probably at first was named bob-tailed cat, which later was shortened to bobcat. The bobcat has stiff-looking tufts at the side of his cheeks. You might think of them as long sideburns, while the lynx has large tufts at the base of his cheeks. The tufts give the impression of bigness which may be one reason why the bobcats and lions face their foes.

The bobcat is somewhat smaller than the 40 pound lynx and weighs from 15 to 25 pounds. The bobcat has smaller paws, probably because it lives in a milder climate and therefore does not need snow shoes. Some male bobcats are about 32 to 50 inches long while the lynx is from 36 to 50 inches long.

The bobcat's coloring ranges from a reddish brown with dark brown spots to a pale yellowish tan with light brown spots. The undersides are whitish. Some bobcats are grayish tan with dark markings. The bobcat's five to seven-inch-long tail is dark on top but white underneath.

The bobcat looks very much like the lynx, but it has shorter ear tufts. Because most bobcats live in a milder climate than the lynx, they have shorter hair. However, when bobcats live in the snow country, their coat becomes thicker and slightly longer.

When chasing hares, which constitute its main diet, the cat catches up with the hare, swipes it into the air, knocks it down, and kills it. Occasionally, it will kill a young or sick deer by leaping down on them from the branches of a tree. Bobcats and pumas have made enemies of ranchers because they will steal chickens, as well as young lambs and calves.

(San Diego Zoo)

Domestic Cat Breeds

We do not know exactly from which species of wild cats the domestic cat evolved, but it is believed that the ancient Egyptians were the first people to domesticate the cat and their choice was probably the African wildcat, *Felis libyca*. This cat has a shorthair coat with markings similar to the European wildcat, *Felis sylvestris*, which at one time was thought to be the wild ancestor. Both of these species have coat patterns resembling the American Shorthair Mackerel Tabby which is striped somewhat like a mackerel. The word tabby can mean any marked cat either a show or ordinary domestic cat but especially, a female one. A tabby has black, brown, or red stripes, bars, streaks, spots, blotches, or flecks on a gray, buff, or brownish-red ground. From the originally domesticated stock has grown a huge population of domestic cats that now includes many breeds.

Founded in 1906, the Cat Fanciers' Association was organized to encourage an interest in purebred cats. A purebred cat is the result of mating cats of the same breed for many generations. One of the functions of this association is to keep a record of these cats and their litters. In fact, the Cat Fanciers Association is the largest registering organization for cats and has registered almost 36,000 of them. Each registered cat has a pedigree or list that gives the name of its parents, grandparents, great-grandparents, and great-great-grandparents, most of which have also been registered.

The Cat Fanciers' Association has rules and regulations concerning cat shows and has compiled a list of the qualifications for each breed. The list gives the acceptable standards by which the cats are judged. These include the weight, length, shape of body, head, tail, position of ears, color, markings, coat condition, and the special characteristics of each breed.

The twenty-three or more breeds of show cats, which have been registered by the Cat Fanciers' Association, are divided into four categories—Natural Breed, Established Breed, Hybrid Breed, and Mutation.

The Natural Breed is made up of cats reproduced by mating like-to-like, in other words, breeding a Siamese to a Siamese. This group contains the Abyssinian, American Shorthair, Egyptian Mao, Japanese Bobtail, Maine Coon, Manx, Persian, Russian Blue, Siamese, and Turkish Angora.

An Abyssinian has short, thick fur. Each hair is ticked with bands of two or more colors. There are two varieties and both are reddish in color. One has ruddy brown fur and each hair has two or three bands of black or dark brown. The other has a rich copper-red fur and each hair has two or three dark copper bands. This cat has been thought to look like those of ancient Egypt.

However, the Egyptian Mao looks somewhat similar to the picture of a spotted cat painted about 3,500 years ago upon the wall of an Egyptian tomb. In 1953 some shorthair spotted cats from Egypt were imported

ABYSSINIAN   (Gale M. Adler)

AMERICAN SHORTHAIR · (Gale M. Adler)

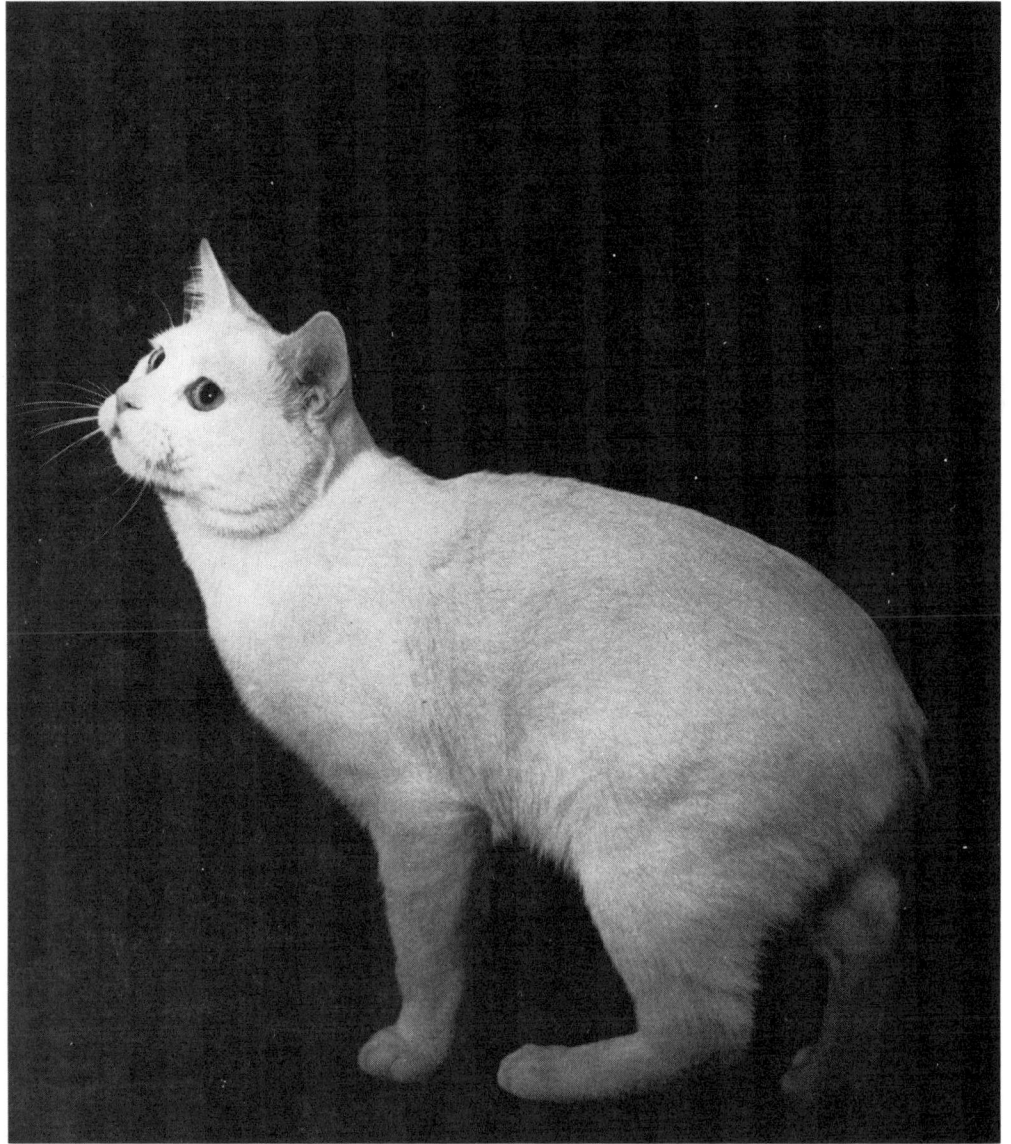

MANX · (Gale M. Adler)

into America and it is from these cats that the Egyptian Mao breed was developed. The markings are in black on gray and in bronze on a tawny-colored coat.

The ancestors of the American Shorthair probably came to America with the Pilgrims. Since then, this cat has been a help in keeping down the rodent population. Its short, stiff, thick coat of fur comes in all colors and combinations except the Siamese color-points pattern. There is a slight difference in body structure between foreign shorthair cats, such as the Siamese and the American shorthair. The foreign shorthair has a long, slender body, legs, and tail. The head is wedge-shaped. The American Shorthair has a muscular, medium to large body, sturdy legs and tail, and the large head is round.

The Manx cat comes from the Isle of Man, which is off the west coast of England. One thinks of a Manx cat as being like a wild bobcat with little or no tail. Only the tailless Manx is accepted in cat shows and there is just a hollow or dimple where the tail would ordinarily be. All manx cats have arched backs, short front legs, long hind legs, broad chests, and round rumps. The coat may be in any color or combination.

Imported from Siam (now called Thailand) about a hundred years ago, the Siamese cat has become the most popular show cat. The cat has four accepted colors, namely: Seal Point, Chocolate Point, Blue Point, and Lilac Point. The colored points are the head, mask or face, ears, tail, legs, and feet. The Seal Point is a rich dark brown on a light cream-colored body. The Chocolate Point is a milk-chocolate brown. The Blue Point is a bluish gray on a snow-white body. The Lilac Point is a pinkish gray on an off-white body. Siamese are sleek, fine-boned, with a wedge-shaped head and blue, almond-shaped eyes. Although these cats at times are very noisy in their demand for attention, their owners believe they have more character than other breeds.

The Persian cat, considered the most beautiful of all the longhaired cats, is the second most popular show cat. The extra-long, flowing, silky, thick fur is unsurpassed. The head is round, the ears small

PERSIAN

(Gale M. Adler)

SIAMESE

(Gale M. Adler)

and far apart, the eyes are large, the nose is stubby and broad. The cat has short legs, a broad chest, and wide shoulders, and the tail spreads out like a plume. The immense ruff continues in a biblike frill between the front legs. The cat is quiet, sedate, and quite regal in appearance. The Persian can be white, black, gray, or have tabby markings. When it has tabby markings, the ground color can be any of the solid colors with the markings in the same but darker color. There are some Persians with large areas or streaks of black, red, and pale orange-red, called tortoiseshell long-hair. Those Persians with patches of black and orange-red, on a cream ground are called sometimes calico or Tortoiseshell and White long-hair— there is also a Tortoiseshell and White Short-hair breed.

The Established Breed is one which was originally created by mating two or more different Natural Breeds together until the bloodline was developed. The breed has since been bred like-to-like. This group consists of the Balinese, Birman, Burmese, Havana Brown, and Korat.

KORAT   (Gale M. Adler)

(Gale M. Adler)

The Korat was found in the northwesterly province of Korat in Thailand and was called by the natives Si-swat which means "the cat with the color of a certain kind of silver-blue seed." The solid gray-blue coat must not have white spots, called "lockets" or "buttons." Although the cat was imported into England and was exhibited at a cat show in 1896, the cat did not come to America until sometime between 1930 and 1940. Even today there are not many of them at cat shows.

The Colorpoint Shorthair is a cross between Siamese and the American Shorthair. This cat has the body shape of the Siamese but instead of the solid color points, the whole cat is mottled and striped. The legs, face, and ear markings are darker than those on the body. Breeders have experimented and have produced colors other than the four classic Siamese colors. They added a red or orange and mixed the colors so that the points are mottled with combinations of one or more contrasting colors.

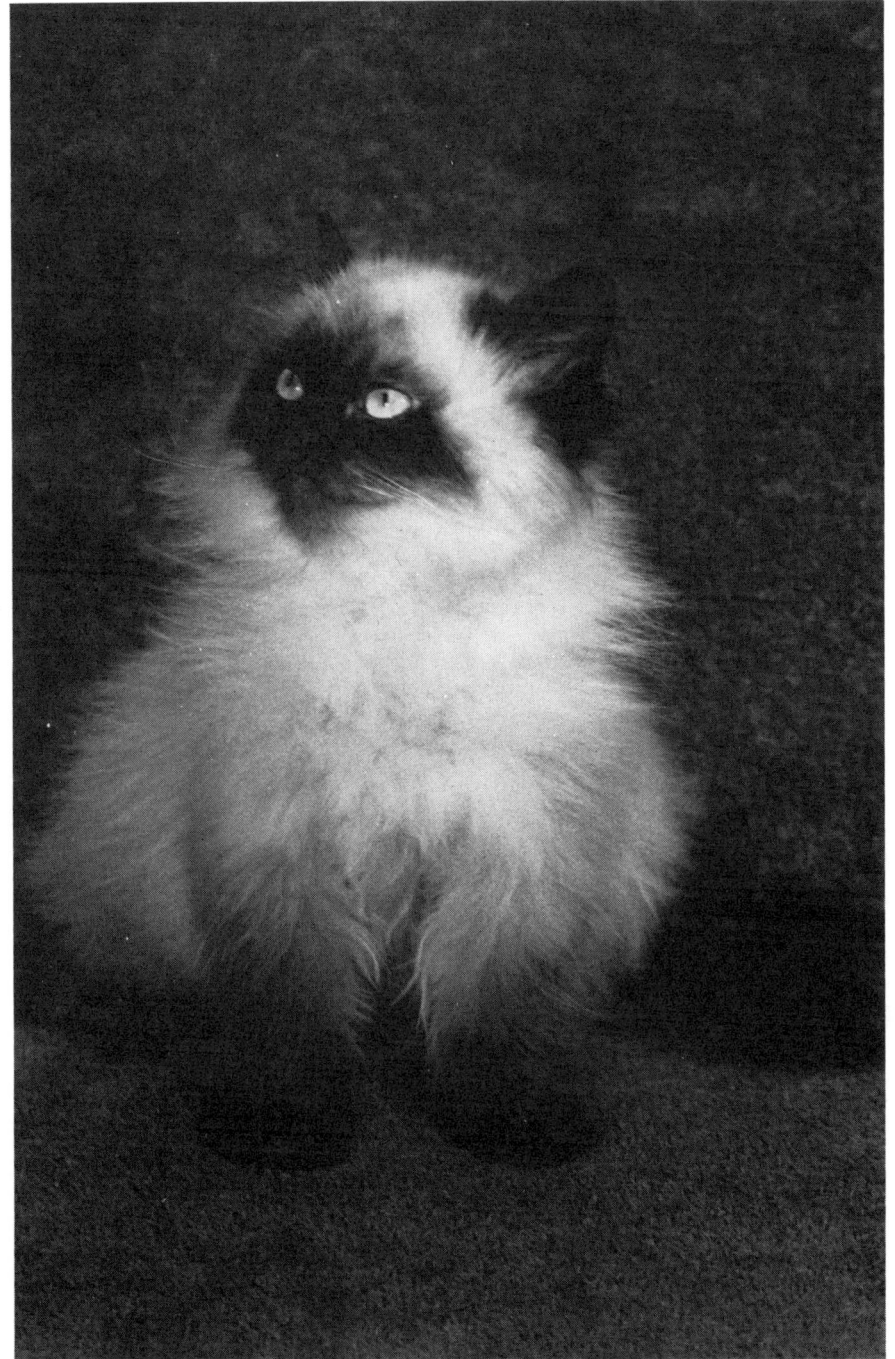

HIMALAYAN

The Himalayan, a cross between the two most popular breeds—the Siamese and the Persian, has become the third most popular breed. Its coat is quite long. However, the end of the longish tail does not taper to a point but is stubby and looks almost as though it had been cut to make the end hairs even.

(Gale M. Adler)

A Mutation is the result of a basic alteration of the physical body. You might think of it as a kind of freak of nature, such as the kinky curls of the Rex cat. In 1950 the first Rex was found in Cornwall, England. He was mated to his mother and the kittens were interbred to produce the bloodline of the Cornwall Rex. The coat is thick, short, and very soft. Ten years later another Rex appeared in Devon, England, and also was bred to produce a bloodline. The Devon Rex is recognized as a separate breed from the Cornwall Rex. In an experiment the two Rexes were mated but because they did not have the same type of genes the result was a litter of normal shorthair kittens. The Devon Rex's coat is thinner, and his whiskers and eyebrows are crinkled. Both Rexes can be any color.

(Gale M. Adler)

Behavior

Domestic cats react very much in the same way as their wild ancestors. This can be noticed in the play of kittens and in their behavior towards their mother. Kittens from birth are groomed by the mother and this act is usually followed by feeding. The two are associated with a sense of well-being and pleasure. Kittens knead or press their mother's nipples to facilitate the flow of milk and this becomes an automatic gesture of affection. Cats expressing happiness will "knead bread." Usually this is done in their owner's lap whether the cat is lying, sitting, or standing. The front paws go up and down to the accompaniment of loud purring.

A cat upon meeting another cat may be apprehensive as to whether it is friend or foe, but each cat can pretty well tell what the other's attitude is by its body movements. When meeting a friendly cat, its mother, or another kitten, the cat will approach with its tail held vertically. Then it will rub its

(Gale M. Adler)

(Gale M. Adler)

cheek, head, or side of its body against the other cat or they may both greet by nose touching, or cheek rubbing. An affectionate greeting can be followed by a period of mutual grooming—the cats licking off dirt, seriously cleaning each other.

When greeting its owner or trying to attract attention to itself, the cat, with its tail vertical, rubs its head or face against the owner's hand or rubs the side of its body against its owner's leg. This is often done to the accompaniment of special greeting sounds which are followed by a period of "kneading bread" and purring.

When another cat or dog is menacing it, the cat reacts by taking the defensive threat pose. With bristling fur the cat stands sideways, arches its back, folds back its ears and stiffens its legs to make itself look larger than normal. The pupils of its eyes are dilated by apprehension and fear. The cat may even bare its teeth, hiss, and growl. However, this mainly indicates that the cat is afraid and will run away rather than fight.

The offensive threat pose means the cat is self-assured and is willing to fight. The

(Gale M. Adler)

pupils of its eyes are contracted. Two cats face and stare at each other head-on. They may hiss, and "scream" excitedly while they flick or twitch their tails from side to side but will remain in this position until they start fighting or one becomes intimidated and retreats.

Although cats have become domesticated, they still have many behavior patterns of the wild. Each male cat has its own territory and marks it by spraying it with urine and at the same time spraying an excretion from a scent-gland located near the tail. Like the cat in the wild, the domestic cat backs up to the object to be sprayed, lifts its tail up and for one or two seconds ejects a stream of urine along with an excretion of the scent gland. This can be very annoying when it is done indoors, especially upon upholstered sofas, chairs, beds, or curtains, because it leaves a very strong, disagreeable odor. Spraying has no connection with the act of urinating—they are entirely separate.

Of course, domestic cats do not have to depend upon their ability to hunt since they are fed regularly by their owners. Neverthe-less, the age-old habit of marking territory persists, and although the cat may not hunt, at least the male will patrol and defend his territory.

The farm cat teaches her kittens how to hunt by example. When the kittens are old enough she takes them with her, and they learn by watching. After they are six weeks old the kittens begin to use in their play different hunting techniques, such as stalking, swiping, leaping, and biting. If the kittens are playing with a ball, a toy mouse, or a rumpled piece of paper, they will go through the stalking movements before they are ready to pounce and bite, or swipe it with a paw.

The play sequences may be interrupted by social interactions, such as fighting or affectionate grooming. One movement that is meant to be an invitation to play is that of lying down on the side, or rolling over onto the back.

Whatever movements the kittens use, they are graceful, sometimes a little clumsy when very young but on the whole entertaining. One wonders who is having more fun—the kitten, or you, the watcher.

(Gale M. Adler)

Not only are there clubs for almost every breed of show cat, there are organizations which devote time and energy to the care and welfare of cats. One of these leading nonprofit organizations is Pet Pride, Inc. It is operated somewhat in the same manner as the American Society for the Prevention of Cruelty to Animals. But, at Pet Pride the lost or abandoned cats are spayed or neutered and then, if a home cannot be found, they are kept at the shelter for the rest of their lives. The shelter has a capacity to house 270 or more cats at one time.

AUTHOR BIOGRAPHY

Harriet E. Huntington was born of New England parents in Florida and developed her love for books and writing in her father's large reference library. Her family moved to California when she was quite young. After her father died, she and her mother traveled extensively—several times to Europe and twice around the world. After a brief stay at Briarcliff College and a nursery school training course at Broadoaks College (now Pacific College in Pasadena), she began her career as a children's book author with *Let's Go Outdoors* and *Let's Go to the Seashore*. These books were written in response to the many questions that children had asked her about nature and the outdoors. She learned photography by trial and error. But now, with more than a dozen books behind her, she has become a nationally known author and photographer.